SPECTACULAR SYDNEY

Magnificent panoramic views of Sydney

KEN DUNCAN
PANOGRAPHS®

Produced completely in Australia

▲ Sunrise, Bronte Beach.

WHAT IS A PANOGRAPH®?

A Panograph is a panoramic photograph, by Ken Duncan, which captures the essence
of a place and a moment in time, to allow the viewer a presence with the image.

▼ Pelicans on the Georges River, Taren Point.

INTRODUCTION

SPECTACULAR SYDNEY, the birthplace of European settlement in Australia, was founded only 200 years ago. Transported to the colony for crimes as petty as shoplifting, convicts were plentiful. Their labour was used to build roads, houses and elegant public buildings, many of which are still evident today, providing a constant reminder of our convict heritage.

Those pioneers instrumental in developing the colony were a hardy breed. Accustomed to an English climate and lifestyle, they initially found their new environment difficult to bear. But from this harsh and hostile land they began to carve a nation; a new frontier where men are measured more by their efforts than by their background.

Sydney is, without doubt, one of the most beautiful harbour cities in the world. Golden beaches, sapphire seas and the rivers which flow from The Great Dividing Range down into the city's sparkling bays, create a crown of natural beauty in which this jewel is set.

▼ On the beach at Bondi.

THANK YOU

I wish to offer my sincere thanks to the sponsors who have endorsed this project as it is only through their support and assistance that we have been able to produce Spectacular Sydney as a truly Australian product.

ANA Hotel Sydney – one of the world's most efficient and environmentally friendly hotels, provides world class comfort and service combined with that personality and character which sets Australia apart from the rest of the world. Telephone: 02 250 6000.

Hanimex / Fuji – there is no better film than Fuji to capture the colours of Australia. Sydney Telephone: 02 938 0400.

Southbank Book – a comprehensive Australian book printing group.
Telephone: Melbourne 03 646 2333
            Sydney 02 964 9546.

Spicers Paper – are committed to keeping printing in Australia by supplying quality papers at internationally competitive prices. Sydney Telephone: 02 534 5544.

Vision Graphics (Processing) Pty Ltd - The Kings of colour film processing in all of Australia. Sydney Telephone: 02 929 8658.

Colour separations by **Laser Graphics (NSW) Pty Ltd.** Sydney Telephone: 02 436 2171.

With love and gratitude to Almighty God and to my parents Jim and Neta Duncan.

Aerial view of Manly. ▶

Overleaf – Royal Easter Show, Sydney Showground.

4

Cities are busy places with an abundance of people, opportunities, choices and pressures. It is easy to move so fast that we lose sight of the beauty that surrounds us. Our peripheral vision can become obscured if we focus only on our goals. City living is the antithesis of outback living, but both have the same foundation – earth.

We must be careful to pause from time to time to appreciate the beauty of God's creation, in order to maintain a healthy balance in our lives and to see ourselves clearly in relation to the whole of creation.

◀ Upper Gledhill Falls, Ku-ring-gai Chase National Park.

▼ Leopard, Taronga Zoo, Mosman.

Previous page – Evening glow over The Rocks and Sydney Harbour.

▲ A glorious start to a new day, Bondi Beach.

The elephant enclosure at Taronga Zoo, with Sydney Harbour in the background.

A lovely view of Sydney for these giraffes at Taronga Zoo.

The Bubble Man at Paddington Markets entices people to buy his wares by floating huge
soap bubbles high above the crowd.

Street performers, Zip and Zap, entertain the crowds at Paddington Markets.
Here Zip shows his skill at juggling fire sticks.

Basking in the winter sun at Balmoral Beach.

Frolicking in the surf at Bondi Beach.

▲ Surf life-savers training on Bondi Beach, ready to provide assistance to any swimmers in difficulty.

◄ An aerial view of Bondi, one of Sydney's most famous beaches.

Overleaf – A humble home and market garden at Kyeemagh provides a stark contrast to city towers on the horizon behind. 23

Classic Australian architecture, Five Ways, Paddington.

Charming inner city terrace houses, Darlinghurst.

Barrenjoey Headland, showing Palm Beach with open ocean to the left
and the safe haven of Pittwater to the right.

Balmoral, a beautiful sheltered beach within Sydney Harbour.
City buildings can be seen rising in the background.

▲ The afterglow of a setting sun colours the evening sky over Sydney.

34

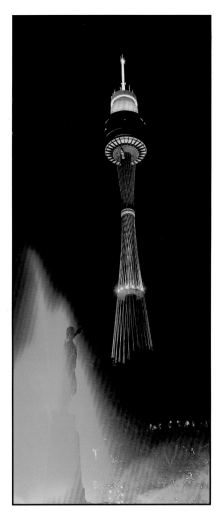

▲ Centrepoint Tower pierces the night sky behind Sydney's Archibald Fountain.

◄ A street vendor sells his fruit and vegetables amid the hustle of Sydney's night life in Kings Cross.

Overleaf – Early morning, Warriewood Beach.   35

Fort Denison, originally built by convicts for the defence of Sydney Harbour.

"The Bounty" sails around Sydney Harbour providing an elegant link with our past.

▲ (Top) Twilight glow upon the sails of Sydney Opera House.

▲ Speeding Ferry, Sydney Harbour.

◀ Gladesville Bridge over the Parramatta River.

A grand old Moreton Bay fig tree in Marine Parade, Double Bay.

Sydney Heads, the entrance to Sydney Harbour, from Dobroyd Head.

El Alamein Fountain, Kings Cross.

Inside St. Phillip's Church, York Street, Sydney.

▲ The Royal Clock, Queen Victoria Building.

◀ Hailed as one of the most beautiful shopping centres in the world,
The Queen Victoria Building, Sydney, was originally designed to
resemble a Byzantine Palace.

51

The historic site of Bare Island, La Perouse, Botany Bay.

Fairlight Pool, with Sydney Harbour entrance in the background.

▲ *(Top)* Crystal Falls, Church Point.

▲ Lord Nelson Hotel, The Rocks, established 1842.

▶ Government House, Sydney.

Looking south across Whale Beach.

Looking west across Bronte Beach and Tamarama.

▲ Barrenjoey Lighthouse flashes its warning to passing vessels as the sun rises over Palm Beach.

The colourful spectacle of Darling Harbour at night.

Previous page – Harbour Bridge and Opera House from Lady Macquarie's Chair.

Looking over Darling Harbour at twilight from Pyrmont Bridge.

An intense challenge draws a crowd to Hyde Park Chess.

Old friends enjoy a quiet game of chess in Hyde Park.

Archibald Fountain, Hyde Park.

Berowra Waters Ferry Crossing.

Pathway to Mona Vale Beach.

Macquarie Lighthouse, Watsons Bay.

▲ The sun rises over fishing boats on Cooks River with Sydney Airport in the background.

▲ The majestic spire of Sydney's Town Hall.

▶ The historic Queen Victoria Building in the heart of Sydney.

75

An aerial view to the east across McMahons Point and North Sydney.

An aerial view of Cronulla and Gunnamatta Bay, Port Hacking.

▲ (Top) North end of Avalon Beach.

▲ Sailing on Sydney Harbour.

◀ A brilliant sunrise at Maroubra Beach.

Sydney's Monorail crossing Pyrmont Bridge, Darling Harbour.

The Spit Bridge opens several times each day to allow boats to pass through.

The golden sun rises majestically over Sydney. Darkness is banished as the warming rays search the city. A new day has begun, bringing with it fresh hope and a wealth of possibilities.

◀ Sea pool, Coogee Surf Lifesaving Club.

▼ Fishing at Bennelong Point.